THE
IRISH FAMINE

CONTENTS

Written by Gail Seekamp and Pierce Feirtear

Collins Educational

An imprint of HarperCollinsPublishers

The Irish Famine 1845-1851 was a major European disaster. It led to the deaths of 1 million people and forced another 2 million to leave Ireland for other countries.

Ireland in 1845

Atlantic Ocean

Irish Sea

Malin Head

DONEGAL

ULSTER

Londonderry
LONDONDERRY

TYRONE

ANTRIM

Lough Neagh

Belfast

FERMANAGH

ARMAGH

DOWN

MONAGHAN

Achill Island

Ballina

SLIGO Sligo

CONNAUGHT

MAYO

LEITRIM
Mohill

CAVAN

ROSCOMMON

LONGFORD
Strokestown

MEATH

LOUTH

GALWAY

Galway

WESTMEATH

KINGS COUNTY

LEINSTER

DUBLIN
Dublin

R. Fergus

Ennistymon

CLARE Limerick

QUEENS COUNTY

KILDARE R. Liffey

WICKLOW

Kilrush

LIMERICK

KILKENNY

CARLOW

KERRY

Kantusk

TIPPERARY

MUNSTER

Waterford

WATERFORD

WEXFORD

CORK Dungarvan

Cork

Schull Skibbereen

- - - - - Province boundaries
· · · · · County boundaries

0   100 miles

0   160 Km

2

The Coming of the Blight

The first news

Early in August 1845, an unexpected letter arrived on the desk of the British Prime Minister, Sir Robert Peel. It told him of a strange disease which had hit the potato crop on the Isle of Wight. Though nobody realised it then, this letter was the first word that the blight, a new potato disease, had arrived in Britain from North America.

Reports of the damage to the Isle of Wight crop had also reached Dr John Lindley, editor of the *Gardeners' Chronicle* and Professor of Botany at the University of London. It did not worry him too much. On 16 August, he wrote that "a blight of unusual character" had appeared on potatoes in the island, and asked readers to send any information they had about it. Just a week later, the *Gardeners' Chronicle* ran a far more dramatic story:

A fearful malady has broken out among the potato crop. On all sides we hear of the destruction. In Belgium the fields are said to be completely desolated. There is hardly a sound sample in

Blight on a potato leaf

Covent Garden market… As for cure of this distemper, there is none… We are visited by a great calamity which we must bear.

The threat to Britain was serious because hard times and high grain prices were forcing ordinary working people to turn to potatoes, instead of bread, as a main source of food. In Ireland, over 3 million people lived almost entirely on potatoes. For them, a crop failure could mean a disaster.

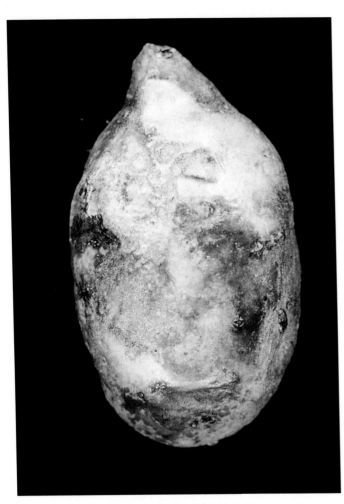

A potato infected by blight

The blight hits Ireland

David Moore was the Director of the Botanic Gardens in Dublin and a regular reader of the *Gardeners' Chronicle*. He had read Lindley's report on the new disease and was keeping a close eye on the potato plot in the Gardens. On 20 August, he noticed that the leaves of the plants were turning black and withering. He feared that the terrible blight had arrived in Ireland.

News of the outbreak was carried in the Dublin *Evening Post* on 6 September. Within days, there were similar reports from around the country. By mid-October every county in Ireland had been affected.

Back in London, the Government had become alarmed. It set up a Scientific Commission to study the problem and discover how the potato could be saved. Dr Lindley was sent to Dublin, where he joined forces with Dr Robert Kane, a local scientist. After some hurried research, they estimated that half the potato crop in Ireland had been destroyed. They published advice on how people could make best use of diseased potatoes, and on how to stop the blight from spreading.

Unfortunately, their advice proved useless. Nothing could be done to stop potatoes from rotting into a foul-smelling mush.

The Cause

What had caused the disease? How had it spread so rapidly? Like most scientists, Lindley believed that bad weather was the cause. He believed that the potatoes had become laden with water as a result of the heavy rain, and that a wet rot had set in. He dismissed suggestions that a fungus might be responsible for the disease, even though he had actually seen such a growth on blighted potatoes. He argued that the fungus was the result of the rot, not the cause.

Sadly, he and his colleagues were mistaken. Fifteen years later, it was discovered that a fungus, *Phytophthora infestans*, had caused the potato blight.

The fungus, a microscopic organism, first appeared as a whitish growth on the decaying leaf of the potato plant. It was barely visible to the naked eye, but under a microscope, it was seen as a great branching network of filaments or tubes. Each tube contained the countless spores which enabled the fungus to reproduce itself rapidly. Once a single spore settled on a leaf, it spurted into growth, sending out its slender tubes to every corner. The destruction moved with lightning speed: within hours an entire field of potatoes was infected!

The spores were carried through the air in tiny droplets of moisture. When the weather was warm and moist, as it was in Ireland in the summer of 1845, everything was set for the spread of blight.

THE CURE FOR BLIGHT

Walking by a vineyard in France one day in 1882, a Mr Millardet noticed that the grapes close to the roadside had remained free of attacks by blight. The roadside grapes had been sprayed with a mixture of copper sulphate and hydrated lime so that people wouldn't steal them. By 1885 Mr Millardet had also developed an effective treatment for blight.

That was forty years too late for the millions of Irish poor whose precious potato crop had rotted overnight in that fateful autumn of 1845.

THE BACKGROUND TO THE FAMINE

The Love of My Heart

Grá mo chroí na preátaí
Nach n-iarann áith nó muileann
Ach a mbaint ins a' gharraí
Agus a bhfágáil ar a tine

Potatoes are the love of my heart.
They don't require a kiln or a mill,
Only to be dug in the field
And left on the fire.

This old Gaelic verse expresses well how the Irish people felt about their potatoes many years ago. The potato had been brought back from the Americas in the mid-sixteenth century, almost three hundred years before the Irish Famine. At the start, it was eaten just by the wealthy. Sir Walter Raleigh, the explorer, grew the potato on his farm in County Cork in the province of Munster in the 1580s but it became everyday food in this most southern of Ireland's four provinces a century before the famine. It spread north and westwards, but was grown mainly on inferior land and eaten by poor people.

By 1800, most of Ireland's small farmers and cottiers, the landless labourers, had switched from oatmeal to the potato as their main food. They had good reasons for doing so. The potato suited Ireland's wet, cool climate, and grew even in the worst soil. It was also nutritious. With a little milk, potatoes provided carbohydrates, protein and minerals; but it took many to make a meal.

And what a lot of potatoes the people ate before the famine! The average man consumed 70 potatoes

A meal of potatoes

6

per day; the average woman, 55 potatoes; and an 11-year-old child about 40 potatoes. Over 50 years, one man could eat a million potatoes. But it was dangerous to be too dependent on a single food.

Lazy beds and lumpers

Most potato crops were grown in lazy beds, which were fat, parallel lines of heaped earth, running from one end of the field to the other like giant pieces of rope under the soil, but each with a flat top. These ridges were about one metre apart, and the potatoes were planted in them.

Making them was hard work. First the cottiers marked a line into the ground with a spade. Beside that line they heaped another line of manure, plus some lime-rich shells and seaweed if they lived near the sea. Next, digging into the first line, they folded the sods of earth on top of the fertiliser mixture. Then they covered this ridge with earth.

The seed potatoes were planted inside this 'soil sandwich' in April or May, and harvested in late summer.

Archaelogists have found that Irish farmers grew crops in lazy beds up to 5,000 years ago. In the 50 years or so before the famine, however, poor people mainly used them to grow potatoes.

Growing just one type of crop made the cottiers too reliant on their potato harvests. Worse still, from about 1810, many cottiers grew just one type of potato. This type was the 'lumper', probably named because of its lumpy shape. The lumper produced big harvests and needed little manure. An acre could produce 12 tonnes, enough to feed a family of two adults and four children, their cow, a pig and a few chickens for most of the year.

Ireland before the famine

In 1845, Ireland was a rich agricultural country whose farmers, apart from the cottiers, produced more than just potatoes. It exported grain, milk and pork to England, and about 7 million of its 8 million population lived off the land. But the society was very divided. The best land was owned by British and Anglo-Irish families who had huge farms or estates. Sometimes they didn't even live in Ireland, and employed agents to manage the estates for them. Such landowners were known as absentee landlords.

Ireland was also a British colony, which meant that it was ruled by Britain. In 1801, Ireland lost what little political power it had when the Act of Union was passed. This broke up the Irish

Parliament, based in Dublin, and gave control to London. So when famine struck, it was British politicians making decisions about people they hardly knew and, in some cases, had little sympathy for. There was a huge gap – in education, living standards, religion and even language – between the Irish cottiers and their British rulers.

Some British politicians and journalists felt the Irish people were impoverished because they were lazy, and grew a "lazy root" (the potato) in "lazy beds". In fact, growing potatoes in lazy beds was back-breaking work.

Ireland's 1.5 million cottiers were at the bottom of the social and economic pyramid. At the top were the landlords like the Earl of Lucan, who owned 60,000 acres in. They usually divided their estates into big plots, renting areas of up to 1,000 acres to wealthy farmers. These farmers were in the middle of the pyramid. They paid about

A cottier's home: not much more than a shed

£1.50 an acre a year for their land (£76 today) and held it for long periods at fixed rents.

In turn, they subdivided their land into much smaller parcels and rented one-, two- or three-acre plots to tenant farmers and cottiers at about £4 an acre a year (£200 today). Often Irish themselves, these middlemen, as they were known, were hated because they made huge profits from the high rents charged to the poor.

Small tenant farmers might have a pig that could be sold to pay the rent, but cottiers had nothing. Instead of paying cash, they paid rent with labour by toiling in the landlord's fields. Some became bitter. Asenath Nicholson, a young American visitor to the West of Ireland, wrote this in 1845:

The poor peasants, men, women and children were gathering seaweed, loading their horses, asses and backs with it, to manure their wretched little

patches of potatoes sown among the rocks. 'Three hundred and sixty-two days a year we have the potato,' said a young man to me bitterly, 'the blackguard of a Raleigh who brought them here entailed a curse upon the labourer that has broke his heart. Because the landlord sees that we can live and work hard on them, he grinds us down in our ways and he despises us because we are ignorant and ragged'.

It wasn't all misery. Thanks to the potato, men and women could marry young and support a big family on a tiny patch of land. Some girls married at 15, or even younger. Another traveller to the West of Ireland wrote this account in 1824:

If they have turf and potatoes enough, they reckon themselves provided for; if a few herring, a little oatmeal and above all the milk of a cow be added, they are rich, they can enjoy themselves and dance with a light heart when the day's work is over.

But Ireland's population was exploding, especially in the West. In the 50 years before the famine, it doubled from 4 to over 8 million. Cottiers hacked their lazy beds deeper into bog and higher up the mountainside. Land in the *clachans*, communal villages shared by several families, was also divided into ever-smaller plots.

Hard times; hungry people

Life got harder after 1815. Grain prices fell when the Napoleonic Wars ended, and the economy slumped. Landlords and farmers raised rents. Some cut back on extras that they used to give their small tenants, like manure for the potato plot or grazing for the cow. Then, the crops failed in 1816-17, 1822 and several times in the 1830s. The cottiers had faced hungry times, but not famine. When famine did strike, Ireland's poor had nothing to help them survive.

POTATO AS A FOOD

A raw potato is 80 per cent water, but it also contains a lot of nourishment. About 17 per cent is made up of carbohydrates, including 2 per cent of protein, but it also contains calcium, iron, thiamin, riboflavin, niacin and ascorbic acid. When eaten with some buttermilk, the liquid left over after making butter, the potato was almost a complete diet.

10

1845-46
FAMINE LOOMS

The hunger

Blight destroyed a third of the Irish potato crop in the autumn of 1845, reducing it from the expected 15 million tonnes to just over 10 million tonnes. By the spring of 1846, hunger began to bite. Some areas, particularly in the West, suffered more than others. People sold their few possessions – their fishing gear, overcoat, the family pig or cow – to buy food. Some got into debt with the local moneylender, known as the *gombeen* man, who charged high interest.

Desperate for food, many ate rotten potatoes, becoming painfully sick as a result. They rummaged around in the fields for turnips and cabbages, foods that were poor substitutes for the nutritious potato.

Despite hunger and hardship, there was no widespread panic. Few deaths were reported. People believed the Government in London would help if the situation got worse.

Sir Robert Peel, prime minister of Britain when the famine began

Peel's plan

Sir Robert Peel, Britain's prime minister, had been Chief Secretary in Ireland during the crop failure in 1816. He wanted to help Ireland, and thought the best way was to import cheap grain from abroad. There was just one big obstacle: the Corn Laws. These laws kept grain prices in the United Kingdom very high by placing a tariff on imports of foreign grain. Peel wanted to remove these laws.

He met with fierce opposition. English farmers were afraid that grain prices would collapse, and Peel's own party, the Conservatives, was hard set against any change. As the politicians argued, Ireland's famine was pushed into the background.

But Prime Minister Peel had another card to play. Back in November 1845, unknown even to members of his government, he had secretly arranged for £100,000 worth (£5 million today) of Indian corn, or sweet corn, to be shipped to Ireland from America. The deal had been arranged

Indian, or sweet corn, offered as a substitute for potatoes

through London bankers. It was such a well-kept secret that the sweet corn had been in Ireland for ten days before the news broke in early 1846. Peel's idea was simple. He wanted to store the corn in food depots, and distribute it in the spring through local relief committees.

He knew that £100,000 of Indian corn could not replace £3.5 million worth (£175 million today) of potatoes lost in the previous autumn. That was not his intention. He planned to sell the corn at cost price. The potato shortage had pushed up food prices in Ireland, and Peel hoped that selling cheap Indian corn would bring them down again.

Indian corn was nicknamed 'Peel's brimstone' because of its bright yellow colour. It was unpopular at first as most people had never seen it before. Many did not know how to cook it and ate it raw, suffering severe stomach cramps as a result. However, as the famine worsened, crowds flocked to the depots to buy corn at 1 penny per lb

12

(21p per 500g today). Peel's gamble paid off. The release of the cheap Indian corn on the market in the spring of 1846 brought the prices of other foods down. Major famine had been avoided, for the time being at least.

No free food

Why did the Government not hand out free food to the starving population? Today we demand this of governments. Whenever famine strikes, be it in Ethiopia or The Sudan, we expect governments to take immediate action. This usually means giving away free food.

Most people thought very differently in the nineteenth century. At that time, governments strongly believed in the economic theory called *laissez faire*. According to this view, people should be free to do whatever they want to in commerce, with a minimum of government interference and without thinking about the effects on anyone else. Laissez faire held that it was not the government's job to provide aid to its citizens. Above all, this theory argued that governments should allow the free market of goods.

Sir Robert Peel's decision to ship Indian corn to Ireland was not in keeping with laissez faire and was therefore courageous. For that, it deserves

INDIAN CORN

Around 7,000 years ago, American Indians (Native Americans) began selecting seeds from the wild grasses, and over the centuries, cultivated a plant very like the sweet corn of today. No-one in Europe knew about this corn before Columbus made his voyage to America in 1492. By that time, the plant was being cultivated by Indians all over the American continent. They called it maize, a name by which it is still widely known. Since the word corn in Britain meant any kind of grain, the new food was called Indian corn.

praise. But even though his programme looked like government intervention, Peel was careful not to interfere with private enterprise. Indian corn was new to Ireland, so there was no market in it as such, and the Government could not be accused of meddling. Peel's solution worked, for a while.

THE HARVEST FAILS AGAIN

Return of the blight

In the spring of 1846, everyone hoped for a good potato harvest the next autumn. Nearly 2 million acres had been planted, and the plants looked green and healthy at the end of July. Then, disaster struck:

On August 6, 1846 – I shall not readily forget the day – I rode up as usual to my mountain property, and my feelings may be imagined when, before I saw the crop, I smelt the fearful stench, now so well known and recognised as the death sign of each field of potatoes. I was dismayed indeed, but I rode on; and as I wound down the newly engineered road, running through the heart of the farm which forms the regular approach to the steward's house, I could scarcely bear the fearful and strange smell, which came up so rank from the luxuriant crop then growing all around; no perceptible change, except the smell, had as yet come upon the apparent prosperity of the deceitfully luxuriant stalks, but the experience of the past few days taught me that all was gone, and the crop was totally worthless.

This report was made by William Steuart Trench, a land agent, after visiting his own potato field in County Laois (then Kings County). Captain Mann, a naval officer stationed in County Clare in the West of Ireland, tells a similar story:

The whole country had changed; the stalks remained bright green, but the leaves were all scorched black. It was the work of a night. Distress and fear were pictured on every countenance and there was a great rush to dig and sell, or consume the crop by feeding pigs and cattle, fearing in a short time they would prove unfit for any use.

Bad times grew worse when blight struck the second year running. Only 3 million tonnes of potatoes were saved, down from a harvest of 14.8 million tonnes two years before (see table on page 17). Poorer people had already sold what they could to raise money: their heavy coats, the family pig, anything. Now many had nothing left.

Right: failure of the potato crop

In despair, they stole turnips from farmers' fields, and even ate weeds like nettles and charlock. These contained some vitamins, but little else.

Those who lived by the sea were not much better off. Many fisherfolk, thinking the blight would be short-lived, had pawned their tackle and nets. Others, weakened by hunger, were too weak to handle their rowing boats. Families combed the shore for shellfish and edible seaweeds like carrageen moss and dulse. Before long, every beach and rock had been stripped of whatever food they held.

Prices soar

Scarce potato supplies pushed up food prices. Potatoes quadrupled in cost, from 4 shillings and 4 pence per barrel (£10.50 today) in 1844 to 17 shillings and 8 pence (£44 today) in 1846. Alternative foods, such as oats and barley, also shot up in price and poor people could not afford to buy them. William Forster, a Quaker who was investigating conditions in the West of Ireland, wrote:

When there before I had seen cows at almost every cabin and there were besides many sheep and pigs owned in the village. But now all sheep were gone; all the cows, all the poultry killed; not one pig left; the very dogs which had barked at me before had disappeared; no potatoes, no oats, workmen unpaid; patient, quiet look of despair.

The future looked grim. Because the 1846 harvest was so small, the cottiers had no seed potatoes to plant the following spring. They were now dependent on charity, caught in a vicious poverty trap.

The Government falls

Meanwhile, Ireland had lost a friend in London. In July 1846, Peel's government fell. Peel had managed to push through the repeal of the Corn Laws, but his farming supporters were angry and voted against him in the next House of Commons bill.

A new government, led by the Liberal Party, came to power. They, even more than the Conservative Government which had just fallen, believed in laissez faire. They didn't think the Government should intervene in Ireland by supplying free food, even to starving people. Charles Trevelyan, who was in charge of famine relief as Assistant Secretary at the Treasury, believed this passionately.

Trevelyan in power

Trevelyan was a complex man. Deeply religious, he was involved in charitable works for needy people in London. But he felt God had sent the potato blight as an opportunity for "moral and political improvement" in Ireland. In his view, ordinary Irish people and their landlords were lazy and backward. He wanted them to take charge of their own lives, instead of abusing British charity, as he saw it. Sadly, he did not seem to realise how hungry, trapped and desperate his neighbours were.

THE COTTIER'S HOUSE

Cottiers and small farmers lived in simple one-roomed cabins with walls made of stones, floor of clay, and roof of thatch. A turf fire burned in an open hearth, and there was usually no chimney. The whole family slept on a mattress of rushes strewn on the floor. Any animals they owned, usually a cow, a pig, or a few hens, were kept inside at night for security and for the extra warmth they gave.

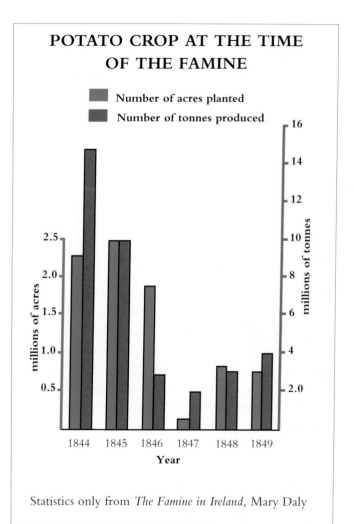

POTATO CROP AT THE TIME OF THE FAMINE

Number of acres planted
Number of tonnes produced

Statistics only from *The Famine in Ireland,* Mary Daly

GOVERNMENT'S RESPONSE

Food depots closed

Despite the general food shortage, Trevelyan decided to stop imports of sweet corn and to close the food depots. Only a few depots in the West were to stay open.

He gave two reasons for his decision. First, he said, providing food at low prices encouraged people to become dependent on the government. Second, cheap Indian corn undercut other types of grain, wiping out the dealers' profits. If they became unwilling to sell grain on the market, the food shortages could get even worse.

The decision caused dismay in Ireland, even among Trevelyan's own officials. Sir Randolph Routh, Chairman of the Relief Commission, wrote to Trevelyan on 14 August 1846. Routh begged him to import food:

> *You cannot answer the cry of want by a quotation of political economy. You ought to have 16,000 tons of Indian corn in the country before Christmas.*

Right: hard labour on relief works in 1898, similar to work carried out during the Famine

Trevelyan did not listen. He cancelled the next shipload of sweet corn, saying, "The cargo of the *Sorcière* is not wanted. Her owners must dispose of it as they think proper."

Public works

Trevelyan believed that public, or relief, works were the best way of tackling the crisis, having proved successful in the past. The hungry masses could be employed on public building schemes and given a small wage with which to buy food.

The works were to be carried out on an even larger scale than before, but organised differently. When Peel was prime minister, the British Government had paid one half the cost of the public works. Under Trevelyan's plan, the entire cost of such works was to be paid by local taxpayers, mainly landlords. The Government would lend them the money, but it would have to be paid back in full within ten years.

Landlords rushed to put in applications for public works in their area. Some were concerned for their tenants, others welcomed the new roads and bridges that would be built. A few acted

under threats from their tenants, like landlords in County Tipperary who got this written warning from a mystery Captain Starlight:

I do hereby require of you to set on work in your neighbourhood or if you will not you will feel the displeasure of me and me brethren (sic).

A food riot by the hungry people of Dungarvan, 1846

The Board of Works was swamped. There were delays in starting projects and paying wages, and people grew angrier as they grew hungrier. "Bands of starving men roamed the country, begging for food, more like famished wolves than men," the historian Cecil Woodham-Smith wrote in her famous book on the Irish famine, *The Great Hunger*. Food stores were attacked, officials beaten up and even murdered. When a public works in Skibbereen, County Cork, was threatened with closure, 1,000 men marched into the town with spades. They were met by soldiers and muskets. The men left quietly when they were given biscuits and a promise that the works would not be halted.

By the end of 1846, there were 500,000 people employed on public works. By spring 1847, the figure had risen to 750,000.

Trevelyan insisted that wages were to be paid only on a piece-work basis; in other words, the amount of money labourers got depended on how much work they did. But many people, weakened by hunger, were not able to do the heavy manual work involved in building roads and piers. Even a fit worker would only earn 8 pennies a day (£1.66 today), and this barely fed a family.

Many workers starved themselves to feed their children. When they fell ill and could work no more, their wives and children took their place. One observer wrote:

It was melancholy in the extreme to see women and girls labouring on the public roads. They were employed, not only in digging with the spade and with the pick, but in carrying loads of earth and turf on their backs and wheeling barrows like men, and breaking stones, while the poor neglected children were crouched, in groups, around the bits of lighted turf.

In one district in County Clare, the West of Ireland, public works were stopped after the supervisor was attacked. A British officer, Captain Wynne, who had been organising the relief there, wrote to the authorities complaining of the hardship this brought on the people:

> *Although not a man easily moved, I confess myself unmanned by the extent and intensity of the suffering I witnessed, more especially among the women and little children, crowds of whom were to be seen scattered over the turnip fields, like a flock of famished crows, devouring the raw turnips, mothers shivering in the snow and sleet, uttering exclamations of despair while their children were screaming with hunger; I am a match for anything else I may meet with here, but this I cannot stand.*

Food exports and riots

While the poor starved, large quantities of grain and meat were being exported from the country. The sight of food leaving the ports was unbearable to the starving, and serious riots broke out. The Government, though, was determined to protect free trade and the supply of food to Britain. Soldiers were sent out into the fields to watch over the harvesting of grain. Food convoys travelled under armed guard. Even grain ships passing up the River Fergus, a small river in the south-west, had a naval escort.

Trevelyan believed that if exports were stopped, the merchants who profited from their sale would then refuse to import foods to Ireland, and the situation would get even worse. He may have been right. But to a starving people, it seemed a cruel and heartless policy.

EFFECTS OF STARVATION

Hunger kills very slowly. Famine victims suffered from many illnesses such as scurvy, caused by lack of vitamin C. This made their gums swell and their teeth fall out. Too little food also resulted in acute anaemia which made people very tired all the time and reduced their resistance to disease. In the last stages of starvation, they got famine oedema which made their limbs and stomachs swell up like sausages because of fluids. This terrible sight can still be seen today when famine strikes anywhere in the world.

SOUP KITCHENS

The winter of 1846–1847 was one of the coldest in living memory. Icy winds blew across the British Isles. In December, huge blocks of ice floated in the River Thames at London. That month, up to 500,000 people toiled on public work schemes in Ireland. Bitter weather and soaring food prices meant they still faced death from cold and hunger. Fuel was expensive. Even if a family could buy vegetables or grain with their wages, they often had no fuel to cook with.

A soup kitchen operated by the Quakers at Cork, 1847

Quaker soup kitchens

One solution was to provide cooked food. By November 1846, soup kitchens, or shops, had been set up in four Irish country towns. These were run by the Religious Society of Friends, or Quakers. The Quakers believed that the stronger and richer should help the weaker and poorer of society. Their numbers were small, but they had close links with Quakers in England and America, from whom help came. They were practical people and some were leaders in business, so they were in a good position to help.

On 23 January 1847, the Quakers opened Dublin's first soup shop on Charles Street, near the River Liffey. The soup was heated by steam in a giant 80-gallon (360 litre) boiler, with heat provided by a furnace in a metal working shop next door. At its peak, this soup shop gave out nearly 1 tonne of nourishing soup per day in two sittings, from 7.30 to 9.30am, and 12 to 3pm. Soup was sold for 1 penny a quart (21p a litre today), or $1\frac{1}{2}$ pence with a piece of bread.

The British Association

As things grew worse in Ireland, some people in England felt they should help. On 1 January 1847, wealthy citizens set up The British Association for the relief of the extreme distress in the remote parishes of Ireland and Scotland. They planned to provide food, clothing and fuel for the needy.

Trevelyan did not think much of the idea. "Feeling in London is so strong against the Irish," he wrote, "that I doubt if much progress will be made in subscription until further horrifying accounts are received." He sent a small contribution, however. The Association raised over £470,000 in all (£23.5 million today), including a £2,000 contribution (£100,000 today) from Queen Victoria, not £5, as many Irish people believed.

Thanks to the Association's work, Trevelyan may finally have realised how big the problem was. "This is a real famine, in which thousands and thousands of people are likely to die," he admitted.

A change of policy

In January 1847, the Government steered a new course. That winter alone, public works had cost

The ticket needed to obtain food at a soup kitchen

£5 million (£250 million today). The Government decided that a cheaper and better way to feed people was through soup kitchens.

Officials were impressed by the Quaker soup shops. They also hoped that supplying pre-cooked meals would keep down food prices, reduce crime and release people from unproductive work, like breaking stones, to grow crops again. The fear was that, if the cottiers did not go back to their fields, they would get too dependent on British charity.

In February 1847, the Government passed the Soup Kitchen Act to set up kitchens all over Ireland. These would give soup away free or sell it cheaply. The Treasury would lend money to set up the scheme, but this would be repaid by local taxes and donations. Irish landlords would also get loans totalling £50,000 (£2.5 million today) to buy seed for their tenants to plant in spring.

The programme didn't work out very well. The soup kitchens were to be run by local committees, but these took months to organise. Despite protests,

Trevelyan decided to shut down public works by the spring, even though 700,000 people depended on them for wages and some towns had no soup kitchen as yet. In fact, soup kitchens were not set up in some places until the summer.

Even Dublin waited until April to get its first soup kitchen. This was set up by a famous French chef, Alexis Soyer, who had created several soup recipes for London's poor. His Number 1 recipe was for two gallons (9 litres), but it is not known how many people this amount fed.

Soyer's Number 1 Recipe

INGREDIENTS

¼ lb (125g) leg of beef

2 oz (56g) dripping (fat)

2 onions and other vegetables

½ lb (250g) flour

½ lb (250g) pearl barley

3 oz (84g) salt, ½ oz (14g) brown sugar

2 gallons (9 litres) water

TOTAL COST:

1 shilling, 4 pence (£3.36 today)

The Model Soup Kitchen serving Soyer's soup was opened with great excitement at the Royal Barracks, Dublin, in a long wooden building that had two doors. When the bell rang at mealtimes, 100 people were let in at a time. They ate their soup at long tables and then they left by the second door. The bowls were washed before the next 100 were let in.

This soup kitchen fed nearly 9,000 per day. By May 1847, 2.25 million people were eating at soup kitchens; in July, when most were finally opened, the number had risen to over 3 million.

'Soupers'

If the soup kitchens had been set up before the bitter winter of 1846, many more lives might have been saved. Even so, the kitchens were not ideal. In some places, evangelical churches gave free soup to gain more members. People who 'took the soup' were expected to change their religion. Those who did so were called 'soupers'. On Achill, an island off the West coast, the Rev. Edward Nangle built a model farm, schools and a hospital during the famine, but he was very unpopular with local people and the Catholic Church because of his attitude. "Fellow countrymen," Nangle wrote in his own newspaper, the *Achill Missionary Herald*,

"surely God is angry with this land. The potatoes would not have rotted unless He sent the rot into them."

Poor people resented charity with strings attached. However, the great majority of Catholic and Protestant clergy gave aid freely, and hundreds of them later died from fever when cholera and typhus struck.

The quality of the soup was another problem. One serving of Soyer's soup gave only one tenth of the calories a person needed each day. At some kitchens, it was so watery or made from such bad ingredients that people suffered digestive problems and died, or became as thin as skeletons.

Weather in the summer of 1847 was glorious. Thanks to the dry conditions, blight barely hit the potato crop. Trevelyan received reports of healthy crops, falling food prices and sunny weather. He ordered the soup kitchens to shut by autumn, and then went on holiday to Europe.

In fact, the potato harvest was a tiny 2 million tonnes. Many cottiers had been too sick or poor to plant a crop that spring, and now faced another winter of starvation. Ireland's problems were far from over.

LANDLORDS' SOUP KITCHENS

Some landlords set up soup kitchens to feed their hungry tenants. The Marquis of Waterford created a soup recipe that was better than Soyer's and told his agents to use it to feed the poor. In December 1846, Lord and Lady Caledon set up three kitchens on their estate, which sold soup and bread "at a very moderate price" each day at 12 noon. The kitchens did not open on Sundays, but served a double helping on Saturdays.

BLACK '47

Crisis deepens

From a report by William Bennett, a Quaker, in 1847:

We entered a cabin. Stretched in one dark corner, scarcely visible from the smoke and rags that covered them were three children huddled together, lying there because they were too weak to rise, pale and ghastly, their little limbs perfectly emaciated, eyes sunk, voice gone, and evidently in the last stage of actual starvation. Many cases were widows whose husbands had recently been taken off by the fever, and their only pittance, obtained from the public works, entirely cut off.

If anything, Ireland's crisis was deepening despite the blight-free potato harvest of 1847. This harvest was not big enough to feed the population. Grain was cheaper, but poor people had no money to buy it. Starvation and disease were everywhere.

Meanwhile, Britain was hit by a financial crisis that autumn, as banks and businesses collapsed. Money was scarce, and there was little cash or sympathy available for Ireland. Charles Wood, the Chancellor of the Exchequer, had written off a £4.5 million debt for famine relief (£225 million today). He refused further financial aid. "The Irish," he wrote, "have had their bellies full of our corn and their pockets of our money." By the first of October, the soup kitchens had closed. Ireland was left on its own to deal with enormous problems.

The workhouse

The Irish Poor Law Act of 1838 had established a workhouse system, similar to the one created in England, Scotland and Wales four years earlier. It was designed to cater for the poorest and most destitute. Over 130 workhouses had been built in Ireland and all were in operation by 1845. As the British Government pulled out of relief operations in 1847, the Irish workhouses had a bigger job than ever. Yet they had little money and not enough staff.

Conditions in the workhouse were very harsh. Meals were of poor quality, inmates were required to perform dreary and monotonous work in return for their keep and families were split up during the day. This explains why just one in three workhouse places had been filled in the period before the Famine.

When famine struck hard, however, the

Searching for potatoes with few to find

The workhouses were designed to house 100,000 people at most, but more than three times as many ended up living in them. The tax money that was collected locally was not enough to cover the costs of running the workhouses. It looked like the programme would collapse. This report on Mohill Workhouse, County Leitrim, December 1847, describes the conditions.

The building we found most dilapidated, and fast advancing to ruin, everything out of repair; the yards undrained and filled by accumulations of filth; fever and dysentery prevailing throughout the house… the paupers defectively clothed… a general absence of utensils and implements… the food given in a half-cooked state – most inadequate… uproar and confusion, the stronger securing an over quantity to the privation of the weaker… no means for the proper treatment of the sick… coffins unused in the internment of the dead.

It was not surprising that so many, especially children, died in the workhouses.

Children in the workhouse

Most workhouse inmates were women and children. By February 1847, children accounted

workhouse seemed to be the only place to turn to. By 1847, they were filled to overcrowding. And still the people kept coming. Captain Kennedy, Poor Law Inspector, described the scene at Kilrush Workhouse in County Clare in November 1847:

The admission to the workhouse amounted to nearly 200 in the past week. Such a tangled mess of poverty, filth and disease as the applicants presented, I have never seen. Numbers in all stages of fever and small pox mingled indiscriminately with the crowd and all clamoured for admission. Their misery and utter helplessness baffles description.

Registered Capstan Mill.

HIVE IRON WORKS

CORK.

for one half of the total 116,000 inhabitants. Some children were orphans, but many had been abandoned by their parents. Some parents went to the workhouse with their children and then fled during the night. They left their children behind, hoping that they would at least be properly fed. In one workhouse in Kanturk, County Cork, the outer walls were raised to 13 feet (4 metres) to keep parents from getting out.

Life was hard for the workhouse children. In Ennistymon Workhouse, County Clare, a boy called Thomas Considine was not allowed milk for two days and had to break stones for an hour each day longer than other workers in June 1848 because he was caught playing cards. Adults and children were put in 24 hours solitary confinement in the dark for other slight offences.

Most children would be in rags by the time they reached the workhouse. On arrival, they were given very simple clothing. Boys often wore a jacket and trousers made of fustian, a coarse-woven fabric, a shirt and a woollen cap. Girls wore a cotton frock, petticoat and cap.

Left: wearying manual work operating a corn grinder in a workhouse

---

WORKHOUSE MENU
for a child under 15
(Ballina Workhouse, 1848)

Breakfast: 4 oz (113g) Indian meal and rice and 1/2 pint (1/4 litre) of buttermilk or molasses.

Dinner: 6 oz (170g) bread and 1 pint (1/2 litre) pea soup for 4 days; 5 ounces rice and Indian meal, and 1/2 pint (1/4 litre) of buttermilk or molasses for remaining 3 days.

Supper: 1/4 lb (125g) of bread or biscuits and 1/4 pint (1/8 litre) of sweet milk or molasses

From: *The Irish Famine: A documentary history,*
Noel Kissane

Killer diseases

Most of the 1 million people who perished during the Irish Famine died of fever rather than hunger. Poverty brought illness and disease. For example, one fifth of the population in the district of Skibbereen, County Cork, died of cholera in a few months between late 1846 and early 1847.

Famine had reduced the population to beggary.

Having pawned their spare clothes, people were left wearing rags. Weakened by hunger, they could not care too much about cleanliness and hygiene. Epidemics of diseases soon came. Typhus was the biggest killer. This disease is passed by lice, though no-one knew that at the time. Aptly nicknamed 'road fever', it quickly spread among the ragged poor who gathered at public works, queued at soup kitchens or crowded into workhouses. After a violent headache, high fever and severe rash, death usually came within four or five days.

Older people were more likely to die from typhus, and children from dysentery. Dysentery causes violent diarrhoea and loss of body fluids. It is caught by drinking polluted water, and is still a major problem in many Third World countries today. In nineteenth century Ireland, however, people didn't know how it was passed on. The weaker people became from hunger, the less likely they were to cut firewood or turf to light fires, and to boil water for cooking. Instead they soaked their food in cold polluted water, not knowing the risks involved.

Lonely burials

Few of the poorest famine victims were buried in graveyards as we know them today. Some were buried in their houses. As deaths increased, bodies were thrown into huge pits, some of them close to the workhouses.

Undertakers often used hinged coffins from which they slid a dead person into a mass grave, so giving them the name of sliding coffins. This way the coffin could be used again and again. Today, many of these burial places are unmarked and barely remembered by local people. Some country villagers turned away famine victims and refused to bury them, for fear of catching diseases themselves.

TYPHUS

Typhus is caused by microscopic rod-like organisms called *Rickettsia*. Lice become infected by these germs and then pass them on to the humans they live upon. *Rickettsia* are named afer the American scientist, Howard Taylor Ricketts, who discovered them in 1910. Ricketts paid for his discovery with his life: he died of typhus a month later, aged thirty-nine.

WIDESPREAD HOMELESSNESS

On 2 November 1847, a dashing young landlord called Major Denis Mahon was shot dead as he returned from a meeting to discuss the local workhouse. That night, it is said, people lit bonfires in the hills near Strokestown Park, his mansion, to celebrate. Tragically, he was one of the more progressive landlords, but desperate times had made the mood in the Irish countryside ugly.

In the autumn and winter of 1847, at least six landlords and around ten farm managers were murdered.

Remember that the soup kitchens, which had fed up to 3 million people a day in the summer of 1847, had all closed by October the first. Hunger and disease were spreading. People were flocking to the workhouses but some were being turned away to die by the roadsides. To make matters worse, families were also losing their homes.

A castle in County Wexford, family home of a wealthy landowner. Homelessness hit more and more of the poor during the famine years

With nowhere to go after being evicted, a family builds a shelter from sods of earth placed over a hole in the ground

The Gregory Clause

The Gregory Clause (1847) was a rule requiring people who owned more than a quarter acre of land to give it up before they could get food by going into a workhouse. Poor people with just an acre or two of land faced the terrible choice of losing their home or of starving more quickly.

Sometimes, kind officials and landlords ignored the Gregory clause. But many landowners were happy to get rid of tenants who had not been able to pay rent for months or years. This often meant they could put the tiny plots of land together and make bigger fields for bigger farmers. In fact, some Irish landlords had pressed for the Gregory Clause in the hope that it would solve their problems.

Trevelyan expected landlords to pay for famine relief. Landlords also had to pay a tax for tenants whose holdings were valued at under £4 (£200 today) per year. So they started evicting poorer tenants to cut their own taxes.

Thousands evicted

In order to evict a tenant, the landlord would obtain permission from the local judge, then call the magistrate. The reason would be non-payment of rent. Then, the landlord's agents would visit the tenant and order the entire family to get out. Resistance was pointless as the landlord's men were usually backed by soldiers and policemen. James Hack Tuke, an English Quaker, wrote this sad account after a journey to the West of Ireland in late 1847:

The policemen are commanded to do their duty. Reluctantly indeed they proceed, armed with bayonet and muskets, to throw out the miserable furniture: dirty time-worn stools and bed-frame, if any, ragged cover-lid [top blanket], iron pot; all must be cast out, and the very roof of the hovel itself thrown down.

Mr Hack Tuke told of seeing up to 700 people being "cast forth, without shelter and without means of subsistence" in his trip. They included

LIST of EVICTIONS, and the Persons Expelled from their Houses, on the Lands of Moveen, the Property of John Westropp, Esq.—*May 15, 1849.*

MOYARTA ELECTORAL DIVISION.

No.	Heads of Families.	No. in Family	Males.	Fem.	Quantity of Land.	Yearly Rent.	Cause of Eviction.	Title.	Observations.
						£. s. d.			
1	Margaret Keane, widow	7	3	4	10 acres	10 0 0	Non-payment.	At will	
2	James Honlehan . .	6	2	4	3 ,,	3 0 0	,,	,,	
3	Lawrence Galvin. .	3	2	1	Cabin	. .	. .	,,	Work-rent.
4	James Meany . .	6	3	3	1 acre	1 0 0	Non-payment.	,,	
5	Felix Meany. . .	6	4	2	Cabin	. .	. .	,,	Work-rent.
6	Michael Scanlon. .	5	3	2	½ acre	0 10 0	Non-payment.	,,	
7	Pat Galvin . . .	6	3	3	Cabin	. .	. .	,,	Work-rent.
8	Martin Downs . .	3	2	1	2 acres	2 0 0	Non-payment.	,,	
9	Mary Scanlon, widow	5	2	3	2 ,,	2 0 0	,,	,,	
10	Joan Flahive, widow.	3	. .	3	Cabin	. .	. .	,,	Work-rent.
11	Catherine Honlihan .	2	. .	2	,,	. .	. .	,,	,,
	John Meany . . .	4	2	2	,,	. .	. .	,,	,,
		7	4	3	4½ acres	3 7 0	Non-payment.	,,	

An extract from an eviction list at Kilrush, County Clare

young and old, well and ill, mothers and children. Evictions of this sort were taking place across Ireland. Some areas were badly affected. In Kilrush, County Clare, some places lost up to a third of their population. By February 1848, a soup kitchen in Kilrush was feeding nearly 10,000 people a day.

Police records indicate that perhaps up to 500,000 Irish tenants – half a million people – were evicted between 1845 and 1854. This was homelessness and hardship on a large scale.

Mahon's violent end

Not all landlords were harsh or greedy people. Some had opened soup kitchens. Some had reduced rents out of sympathy for their tenants. For example, in 1847 the 3rd Earl of Caledon, who had 30,000 acres in the northern province of Ulster, cut rents by up to one half. Others, like Major Mahon, paid the boat fare of tenants who wanted to emigrate.

Mahon was an ex-calvary officer. He had inherited nearly 7,000 acres at Strokestown Park, County Roscommon, just as the famine started, but it already had huge debts. This land had a special history. It had once been owned by an Irish chieftain, but had been confiscated by the British leader Oliver Cromwell and given to the Mahon family in the 1650s.

Denis Mahon found it very hard to collect rents after 1845, partly because his tenants organised a rent strike. His cousin, John Ross Mahon, agreed to act as agent. He suggested that the number of tenants be sharply reduced and the average farm be increased from three to nine acres for growing oats, not potatoes. The Major agreed to this plan, and helped 900 of his landless tenants by paying their fares to Canada in the spring of 1847. Each family was given a small portion of rice, oatmeal and saltfish to take on the long boat journey. Another 3,000 tenants who did not want to leave were evicted in 1847.

The Major was murdered that autumn. Perhaps it was due to the evictions or to reports that many of his tenants had died of fever on the long voyage to Canada. Some believe it was because he quarrelled with the local parish priest on how the workhouse should be run. No-one knows.

Right: an eviction in progress. Often the thatched roof and walls of a house were destroyed after the eviction

Young Ireland and revolt

At around this time, revolutions were sweeping Europe. In February 1848, King Louis Philippe was forced out of Paris by rebels. There were revolts in Berlin, Milan, Venice and Vienna.

In Ireland, a group of men got together and created an organisation called Young Ireland. They founded a newspaper, *The Nation,* which called for complete independence from Britain and ownership of Irish land by Irish people. They spoke of revolution, and were split on the method between those who approved of armed force and those who didn't.

One of the Young Ireland members, William Smith O'Brien, was a landlord himself. In July 1848, he assembled an army of 500 volunteers. They clashed with around 50 policemen, led by an inspector on a horse. There was a brief – some reports say almost comical – showdown at a house owned by a woman called Widow McCormack. It was a very short rebellion. The Young Ireland leaders were tried for treason and sent to Tasmania. But the anger which they and others felt was not gone. John Mitchel, the son of a Presbyterian minister and a founder of Young Ireland, expressed it like this: "The Almighty indeed sent a potato blight, but the English created a Famine."

He may have given only one side of the story, but these strong feelings were widespread and sowed the seeds of Irish revolution.

SCAILPS

After being evicted, cottiers were desperate for shelter. Sometimes they kept the thatch and timbers of their wrecked cabin to build a makeshift home. These huts, called scalpeens, were built in ditches or holes in the ground. Other cottiers could do no more than make a roof from sods of earth and branches over a hole. These were called scailps. Even then, these evicted families were chased away by the law wherever they tried to stay.

EMIGRATION

A long farewell

It was in the year of '46
I was forced to leave my native land.
To old Ireland I bid a long adieu
And to my fond relations all.
But now I'm in America
No rent or taxes we pay at all.
So now I bid a long farewell
To my native land old Donegal.

(A ballad from the time of the Irish Famine)

There was just one escape from the horrors of starvation, disease and eviction. Even before the first crop failure in 1845, people were leaving Ireland to seek a better life in a new country. Famine turned this stream into a flood.

Huge numbers headed for Britain. They were desperate to reach a place where, if they could not find work and a home, they might at least be fed. English Poor Law provided for free food and the English workhouse served sugar, butter, tea, and meat once a week. Even this mean ration was a paradise compared to Irish workhouse food. The fare to Britain was roughly one week's wages on the public works. Emigrants arrived at three main points: the Clyde in Scotland, the ports of South Wales, and Liverpool. They often brought the fever with them.

Liverpool was worst hit by this massive influx of paupers. They filled the workhouses, crowded into the slums and slept on the streets. A city of 250,000 population found itself feeding a further 130,000 people a day on outdoor relief. The city's

A notice of packet ships leaving from Liverpool for New York

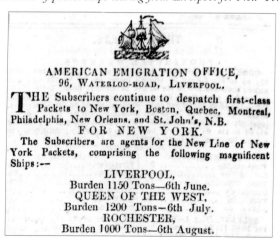

AMERICAN EMIGRATION OFFICE,
96, WATERLOO-ROAD, LIVERPOOL.
THE Subscribers continue to despatch first-class Packets to New York, Boston, Quebec, Montreal, Philadelphia, New Orleans, and St. John's, N.B.
FOR NEW YORK.
The Subscribers are agents for the New Line of New York Packets, comprising the following magnificent Ships:—
LIVERPOOL,
Burden 1150 Tons—6th June.
QUEEN OF THE WEST,
Burden 1200 Tons—6th July.
ROCHESTER,
Burden 1000 Tons—6th August.

38

police could not cope, and 20,000 citizens had to be sworn in as special constables. Then typhus struck, infecting 60,000 people.

The citizens of Liverpool, especially the ratepayers who were forced to cover the costs of running the soup kitchens, begged the Government to act. In May 1847, Parliament rushed through a bill which allowed Liverpool and other cities to send the destitute Irish back home. Once this law came into effect, mass emigration from Ireland slowed almost to a stop.

But the Irish were already setting their sights on another country.

On to the United States

To the Irish emigrant, the United States was a bright beacon of hope in an ocean of gloom. It cost 70 shillings to get there (£175 today). The fare to Quebec, in Canada, was 20 shillings cheaper, so many chose to go there first and then slip across the border to the USA.

Lower fares to Canada meant even poorer travelling conditions. Most of the ships carrying emigrants were cargo vessels carrying corn and

Left: two ships departing for Liverpool from Cork as hundreds of other passengers wait hopefully for the next one

timber one way and passengers the other. They were old and often in dangerous condition. They soon became known as 'coffin ships' due to the number of deaths that happened aboard them.

The *Elizabeth and Sarah* was a typical example. It set sail from Ireland for Quebec in July 1846 with 276 passengers on board. This was 64 more passengers than on the official list. There were just 32 berths and no toilet facilities. Nor was there enough water and food on board. The state of the vessel was, in the words of one witness, "horrible and disgusting beyond the power of language to describe." The voyage, which should have taken a month, was twice as long because the captain took the wrong course. During the journey, 42 passengers died of hunger and thirst. It is estimated that in 1847 one in every six passengers on these coffin ships to Canada died on board or shortly after arrival.

Grosse Isle: a beautiful graveyard

Thirty miles down the St Lawrence River from Quebec lay Grosse Isle, a small and beautiful island, full of trees, shrubs and wild flowers. In 1847 it was the quarantine station for Quebec. Immigrants were kept in isolation here for at least ten days until a doctor gave them clearance to enter the country. The hospital on the island was small, far too small to deal with the crisis which unfolded there that summer.

As soon as the ice melted on the St Lawrence River in May 1847, the first coffin ships began to arrive from Ireland. Each was crammed with its wretched cargo of exhausted, starved and diseased passengers. The *Syria* was the first to arrive on 17 May. Out of its 241 passengers, 84 had typhus. Nine others had already died at sea.

Within a fortnight, a further 40 ships had dropped anchor at Grosse Isle. By that time, there were at least 1,000 cases of fever on the island and an equal number of infected passengers on board the ships. Still more ships arrived. By mid-summer, there was a line of vessels seven miles (11 kilometres) long on the St Lawrence River.

The island was desperately short of beds, medicine, and medical staff. Doctors themselves caught typhus and died, and nobody could be found to replace them. Seriously ill and dying passengers were left for days on board without treatment. Healthy passengers who had been cooped up with the sick also got ill. One ship arrived with 427 people on board. After two weeks of quarantine, two thirds of them were dead.

By the time the St Lawrence froze over again in September, over 5,000 children, women and men had perished.

Today, a small monument marks their burial place on Grosse Isle. Inscribed on the monument are the words:

> IN THIS SECLUDED SPOT LIE THE MORTAL REMAINS OF 5,294 PERSONS, WHO, FLYING FROM PESTILENCE AND FAMINE IN IRELAND IN THE YEAR 1847, FOUND IN AMERICA BUT A GRAVE.

A new life

Most of those who survived made their way south to the USA. They found homes in the slums of the great cities in the east: Boston, Chicago, New York. Life was hard for them there, for they were poor and unskilled. The men worked mainly as labourers, the women as domestic servants. Still they were able to send money home to their relations in Ireland, to enable them to buy a ticket for America. In fact, the total of the money sent back amounted to £1 million (£50 million today) a year.

My dear father and mother, brothers and sisters.

I write these few lines to you hopeing that these few lines may find ye all in as good state of health as I am at present, thank God. I recieved your welcome letter to me dated 22nd of May, which was a credit to me for the stile and elligence of its fluent language, but I must say rather flattering. My dear father, I must only say this is a good place and a good country, for if one place does not suit a man he can go to another and can very easily please himself.

But I can assure you there are dangers and dangers attending comeing here; but, my friends, nothing venture, nothing have. Fortune will favour the brave. Have courage and prepare yourself for the next time that worthy man, Mr. Boyen (Michael Boyen, agent for Crown lands at Kingwilliamstown), is sending out the next lot, and come you all together couragiously and bid adiu to that lovely place, the land of our birth. But alas, I am now told its the gulf of misery, oppression, degradetion and ruin of erry discription, which I am sorry to here of, so doleful a history be told of our dear country.

This, my dear father, induces me to remit to you in this letter 20 dollars, that is four pounds, thinking it might be some acquisition to you untill you might be clearing away from thet place all together, and the sooner the better. For believe me I could not express how great would be my joy at seeing you all here together, where you would never want or be at a loss for a good breakfast and dinner.

your Ever Dear and Loveing Child Margaret

An extract of a letter to the family back in Ireland from an emigrant living in America, dated New York, 22 September 1850. The writer expresses sadness for the fate of the country and people she left behind and looks forward to being reunited with her family (spellings as in the original)

By the end of the Famine three years later, over 1 million people had left Ireland. Within five years the figure had risen to 2 million as more people chose to follow the example of relatives and friends and seek a better life abroad.

Above: a closely packed crowd between decks on an emigrant ship

Left: an emigrant ship embarking from Liverpool for America

AUSTRALIA

In famine times, the fare to Australia was £15 (£750 today), or four times the cost of a passage to North America. The journey took up to four months.

Few tenants or landlords could afford this sort of money. However, the British Government decided to sponsor emigration by paying people's fares in order to get more women to the new colony. Between 1848 and 1850 over 4,000 girls aged between 14 and 18 were sent to Australia on the Orphan and Pauper scheme. Many others were sent as a punishment, sometimes for stealing tiny amounts of food.

The Aftermath

Disease and starvation continued in Ireland till 1851. The potato crop failed again in 1848, but the British Government did little to help. Britain was angry about the Young Ireland rebellion. It considered the Irish ungrateful and was unwilling to give them more aid.

The Quakers did not reopen their soup kitchens, saying the problem was too big for private individuals to cope with. Luckily, thousands of Irish school children still got daily meals from The British Association. The Government spent only another £500,000 (£25 million today) on relief until the famine ended, compared to the £8 million (£400 million today) it had given between 1845 and 1847. Ireland badly needed help, as 1849 was probably the worst year of the famine: nearly 250,000 people died.

In 1851, when life started to return to normal, Ireland was a different and sadder country.

About 1 million people had emigrated, and at least 1 million more had died from hunger and disease. If the potato blight had not struck, the population might have grown to over 9 million. Instead, the 1851 Census recorded that there were just 6.5 million people.

There was huge social change, too. In 1841, nearly 50 per cent of all land holdings had been under five acres. Ten years later, the number of such small farms had fallen to 15 per cent, but the number of bigger farms, consisting of 15 acres or more, had grown.

Many of Ireland's big landlords were bankrupt and would never be as powerful again. The Irish farmers had gained most, because they got more land and power when the cottiers left. But land, and British rule, were still big issues. Michael Davitt, son of an evicted cottier, founded the Land League in the 1880s to fight for land reform. His campaign was very successful. Irish tenants won important rights, and between 1903 and 1920, nearly half of Ireland's 22 million acres changed hands, passing from landlord to tenant.

Reform was not enough for some Irish people. In 1916, a band of revolutionaries staged the Easter Rising with the aim of breaking away from Britain. Five years later, in 1921, twenty-six of Ireland's thirty-two counties were granted independence. Six counties in Northern Ireland remained under British rule.

Much can be learned from Ireland's famine.

Action From Ireland (AFrI) is an Irish charity which was set up to help famine victims in other countries. It argues that famines will keep happening unless we take action. AFrI has helped Irish people to remember their own history by locating and marking long forgotten sites where famine victims were dumped into a common grave. These graveyards of the Irish famine are often just a field.

AFrI declares that it is a "lie" to say that famines are caused by food shortages alone, because Irish people died in a world where food was plentiful. The same is true of Ethiopia and The Sudan today, AFrI says.

Perhaps that is only partly right. The scale of Ireland's disaster was huge, and the British Government and its people spent millions of pounds on famine relief. However, it can be said that the British Government's contribution was not enough. Compared to the £20 million (£1,000 million today) it had spent a few years earlier in compensating West Indian slave owners for freeing their slaves, the £8.5 million spent in Ireland between 1845 and 1851 seems small, to say the least.

Ireland's starving cottiers were victims of harsh circumstances. They did not die just because their potato crops failed. History is more complex, as we have seen. Like a jigsaw, it pieces together the social, economic and political causes of major events, like the Irish Famine or famines today. If we understand and learn from the past, we can shape the future to make the world a better and fairer place.

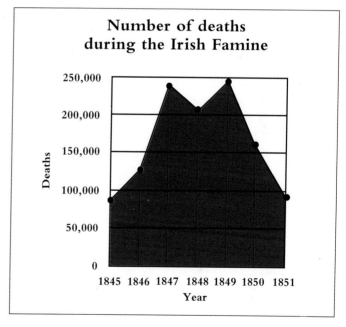

Number of deaths during the Irish Famine

Bibliography

Action From Ireland (AFrI), *Famine is a Lie*, Dublin, 1995

Great Famine Project; Information pack, Dublin

Campbell, Stephen, *The Great Irish Famine*, The Famine Museum, Roscommon, 1994

Daly, Mary E., *The Famine in Ireland*, Dundalgan Press (W. Tempest) Ltd, Dundalk, 1986

Goodbody, Rob, *A Suitable Channel: Quaker relief in the great famine*, Pale Publishing, Bray, 1995

Irish Times, Famine Diary series, Dublin 1995/1996

Kissane, Noel, *The Irish Famine; A documentary history*, National Library of Ireland, Dublin 1995

Littonnes, Helen, *The Irish Famine; an illustrated history*, Wolfhound Press, Dublin, 1994

Nelson, E. Charles, *The Cause of the Calamity: Potato blight in Ireland and the role of the National Botanic Gardens, Glasnevin*, The Stationary Office, Dublin 1995

North Clare History Society, *A Guide to Ennistymon Union: 1839–1850*, 1992

Percival, John, *The Great Famine: Ireland's potato famine, 1845-51*, BBC Books, 1995

Poirteir, Cathal (ed), *The Great Irish Famine*, Mercier Press, Dublin, 1995

Woodham-Smith, Cecil, *The Great Hunger; Ireland 1845-1849*, Penguin, 1991

Further Reading

Gray, Nigel, *Black Harvest*, Collins Educational in the *Plays Plus* series, 1992

Conlon-McKenna, Marita, *Under The Hawthorn Tree*, O'Brien Press, 1991

Pilling, Ann, *Black Harvest: The Terrible Legacy of the Irish Famine*, Collins Educational in the *Cascades* series, 1996

INDEX